D1411045

Profiles in Greek and Roman Mythology

THESEUS

Mitchell Lane
PUBLISHERS

P.O. Box 196
Hockessin, Delaware 19707
Visit us on the web: www.mitchelllane.com
Comments? email us: mitchelllane@mitchelllane.com

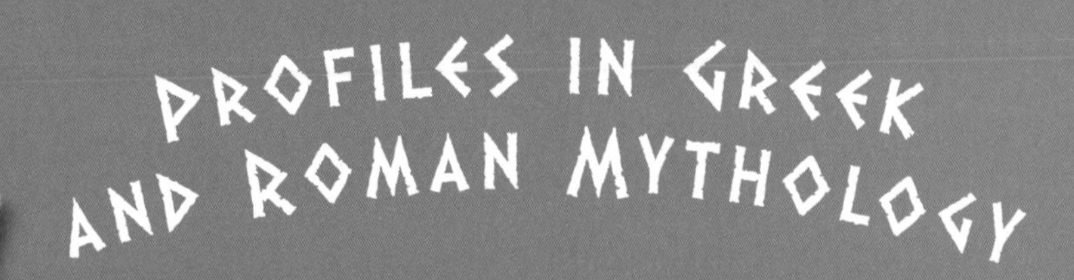

Titles in the Series

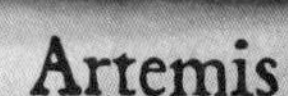

Athena

Dionysus

Hercules

Jason

Perseus

Theseus

Zeus

Profiles in Greek and Roman Mythology

THESEUS

Kathleen Tracy

Mitchell Lane
PUBLISHERS

P.O. Box 196
Hockessin, Delaware 19707
Visit us on the web: www.mitchelllane.com
Comments? email us: mitchelllane@mitchelllane.com

Printing 1 2 3 4 5 6 7 8 9

Library of Congress Cataloging-in-Publication Data

Tracy, Kathleen.
Theseus / by Kathleen Tracy.
p. cm. — (Profiles in Greek and Roman mythology)
Includes bibliographical references and index.
ISBN 978-1-58415-554-6 (library bound)
1. Theseus (Greek mythology)—Juvenile literature. I. Title.
BL820.T5T73 2007
398.20938'02--dc22

2007000773

ABOUT THE AUTHOR: Kathleen Tracy has been a journalist for over twenty years. Her writing has been featured in magazines including *The Toronto Star's* "Star Week," *A&E Biography* magazine, *KidScreen* and *TV Times*. She is also the author of numerous books for Mitchell Lane Publishers, including *William Hewlett: Pioneer of the Computer Age* and *The Fall of the Berlin Wall, Gwen Stefani, Johnny Depp, Kelly Clarkson,* and *Paul Cézanne.*

PHOTO CREDITS: p. 8—Syracuse University; p. 11—Indiana University; p. 14—Jonathan Scott; pp. 6, 12, 16, 28, 35—Barbara Marvis; pp. 20, 30—University of Texas; p. 36—Pierre-Narcisse Guérin; p. 41—George Washington University

PUBLISHER'S NOTE: This story is based on the author's extensive research, which she believes to be accurate. Documentation of such research is contained on page 46. The internet sites referenced herein were active as of the publication date. Due to the fleeting nature of some web sites, we cannot guarantee they will all be active when you are reading this book.

To reflect current usage, we have chosen to use the secular era designations BCE ("before the common era") and CE ("of the common era") instead of the traditional designations BC ("before Christ") and AD (anno Domini, "in the year of the Lord").

PLB

TABLE OF CONTENTS

Profiles in Greek and Roman Mythology

In 1966, the remains of an ancient Greek villa was uncovered in Paphos, Cyprus. Built around the fourth century BCE, it was the largest ever found on Cyprus. Inside the villa were many decorative mosaics, or pictures made with small pieces of colored stones or glass. One of the mosaics showed Theseus killing the Minotaur. As a result, the villa has become known as the House of Theseus.

THESEUS

CHAPTER 1
Battle of Marathon

In 490 BCE, on a hill above the village of Marathon, the Athenian General Miltiades (mil-TEE-uh-deez) readied his troops for battle against the powerful Persians, also called the Medes.

The tensions between Athens and Persia had been brewing for over half a century. After King Cyrus (SY-rus) conquered the country of Lydia (LIH-dee-uh) around 550 BCE, other nearby regions also eventually came under Persian control. Cyrus handpicked new rulers, known as tyrants, for each region. Greeks were required to serve in the Persian army and were also taxed heavily. Persia's King Darius I was determined to rule the entire Aegean region. He was still angry at Athens for destroying Sardis in a revolt nine years earlier. Now, Athens found itself fighting for its very survival.

Darius had assembled an estimated 50,000 soldiers[1] to crush the opposition. Warships and transport vessels filled with infantrymen headed for Greece. When the first Persian ships arrived and conquered the Greek city of Eretria (ayr-EE-tree-uh) in mid-August, it became clear what Darius planned to do.

The Athenian generals sent a courier named Pheidippides (fy-DIH-puh-deez) to Sparta—a distance of around 140 miles—asking for military help. According to Greek historian Herodotus (heh-RAH-duh-tus), Pheidippides, "a runner of long day-courses and one who practiced this as his profession . . . was in Sparta on the next day. . . . It pleased them well to come to help the Athenians; but it was impossible for them to do so at once."[2]

By this time, Miltiades and his 10,000 soldiers were at the village of Marathon, twenty-six miles from Athens. He knew that if he didn't stop the Persians at Marathon, the enemy would march straight to

CHAPTER 1

After leading his troops to victory over the Persians, Miltiades was considered a hero. As a reward, he was given a fleet to command. But after he led an unsuccessful attack on the island of Paros, he was stripped of his command and fined. He later died of wounds received in the battle.

Athens. Rather than wait for the Spartan reinforcements to arrive, Miltiades devised a bold battle strategy. Instead of deploying his troops in the traditional way, leading with the soldiers in the middle of the advancing line, Miltiades' plan called for the soldiers on the wings, or ends, to move forward ahead of the middle. He left only half as many soldiers in the center of the advance as usual in order to cover the whole battle line.

The Greeks' superior armor and the long spear they carried, called a pike, gave them an advantage over the Persians in hand-to-hand combat. But the majority of the Persian soldiers were archers, and their rain of arrows was their biggest threat. Typically, Persian armies would wait for their opponents to advance, then bombard them with arrows.

Miltiades' solution was to simply outrun the arrows. He instructed his men that when the battle began, they should stay in formation until they were about 200 yards from the archers. That was the farthest distance the Persian arrows could travel. Once they were in range of the arrows, the Athenian soldiers were to run full speed at the enemy.

The importance of the battle was clear—a Persian victory would almost certainly bring an end to Greek culture. Defeat was not an option.

Miltiades gave the order to advance. As planned, the wings moved ahead of the center. Suddenly, as several Athenian soldiers would later report, an apparition hovered over the battlefield. It was the ghost of Theseus (THEE-see-us), the legendary king of Athens, running ahead of the Greeks, leading their charge against the startled Persians.

According to Herodotus:

> The Persians, seeing them coming at a run, made ready to receive them; but they believed that the Athenians were possessed by some very desperate madness, seeing their small numbers and their running to meet their enemies without support of cavalry or archers. . . . They were the first Greeks we know of to charge their enemy at a run and the first to face the sight of the Median dress and the men who wore it. For till then the Greeks were terrified even to hear the names of the Medes.[3]

Just as Miltiades had planned, the Persians quickly broke through the center of the line—but what they thought was a rout turned into a slaughter. The outer wings encircled the Persian troops, trapping them. Those who weren't immediately killed broke ranks and retreated, running for their ships. Herodotus described the Greek pursuit:

> As the Persians fled, the Greeks followed them, hacking at them, until they came to the sea. Then the Greeks called for fire and laid hold of the ships. . . . In this fashion the Athenians captured seven of the ships.[4]

Herodotus reports that over 6,000 Persians died in the carnage. Only 192 Athenians lost their lives.

Still hoping to pull out a victory, Darius' brother Artaphernes (ar-tuh-FER-neez) sailed for Athens, assuming the city would be undefended. To his shock, Miltiades had rushed his troops back to Athens in time to prevent Artaphernes from landing and mounting an attack. Thwarted, the Persians sailed home.

The stunning and historic victory marked a turning point for Athens and all of Greece. It instilled a deep sense of pride and set the stage for Athens' rise as the cultural, artistic, and political center of Greek civilization. The soldiers who died were buried on the battlefield, and their mass grave is still visible. For hundreds of years they were hailed as heroes, and the anniversary of the battle was celebrated as a holiday. According to local lore, the sounds of clanging swords can still be heard in the dead of night.

The Battle of Marathon was the first recorded battle and spawned legends that survive to this day, such as the popular belief that Pheidippides ran the twenty-six miles from Marathon to Athens to announce the Greek victory, only to drop dead from exhaustion as soon as he delivered the message. This story was the basis for the modern marathon race. However, there is no historical evidence it ever happened. Herodotus only mentions Pheidippides' run to and from Sparta before the battle. The first mention of a Marathon-Athens run wasn't until nearly 600 years later in Plutarch's *On the Glory of Athens*, a story that was repeated a century later by the Greek writer Lucian.

The victory at Marathon also resurrected a long-forgotten Greek hero who had come to represent Athens' rise as a powerful city-state. The settlements that evolved into Athens were first inhabited during the New Stone Age. Toward the end of the Bronze Age, the Achaeans (uh-KY-uns), or ancient Greeks, migrated from the north. Although archaeologists don't know their exact origin, it is known they were skilled in pottery making, working with metals, and

Ivory statue from Mycenae, dating from the fifteenth century BCE. The city of Mycenae was where the first important Greek civilization emerged. It flourished during the Bronze Age. Many of the Greek myths are set during this time, as are the epic stories *The Iliad* and *The Odyssey.*

agriculture. The first great Greek civilization, the Mycenaean (my-SEE-nee-un), emerged in the Peloponnesus—the peninsula that forms the southern part of Greece on the other side of the Isthmus of Corinth—around 2000 BCE. By 1600 BCE, Mycenae (my-SEE-nee) was one of the most important cities in the ancient world and was

the home of King Agamemnon (aa-guh-MEM-non), who led the Greeks in the Trojan War.

As the Mycenaean civilization advanced, the Minoan civilization on the island of Crete (KREET) was developing. (Crete is off the coast of Greece). Historians believe that the mainland Mycenaeans were greatly influenced by the Minoan culture.

It was during this time that Athens' first kings appeared. Not much is known about them except for legends that have passed down through time. The first king, Cecrops (SEE-krops), was said to be half man and half snake. It was he who chose the goddess Athena (uh-THEE-nuh) as the city's patron: She made the first olive tree grow on the slopes of the Acropolis, the rocky hill where the city first started.

Many historians believe that Theseus was an actual person, but that over the years he was given mythical qualities. He was considered a hero for being the first king to establish democracy in Athens, but over the centuries Theseus had fallen into disfavor. He had been replaced in the minds of Athenians by other heroes. However, when news of the soldiers' claim of seeing his ghost on the battlefield spread, Athenians once again embraced their legendary ruler.

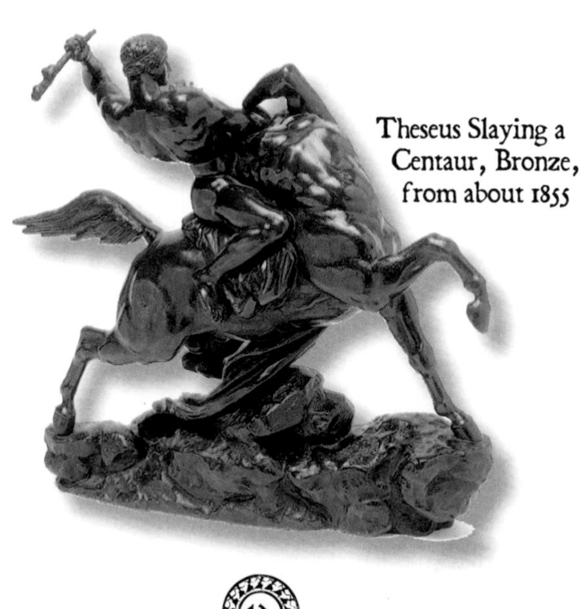

Theseus Slaying a Centaur, Bronze, from about 1855

The Lydians

Statue of Alexander the Great, Thessaloniki

Lydia was founded around 687 BCE by King Gyges (GY jeez), who named Sardis the capital city. The area, originally known as Maeonia, had fertile land for crop growing and rich mineral and metal deposits. The Lydians were the first culture in history to mint coins, making their currency out of gold, silver, and electrum.

Gyges and the kings who followed him conquered much of the Asia Minor coast (in what is now Turkey), which included many of the Greek cities along the Aegean (uh-JEE-un) Sea. But Lydia remained friendly with its territories. Greek men would sometimes fight for Lydia as mercenaries—soldiers who were paid to fight for a country other than their own.

By the time Croesus (KREE-sus) became king in 560 BCE, Lydia had grown into a powerful empire . . . too powerful for the Persians. Seeing Lydia as a threat to its own empire, King Cyrus the Great sent troops to Lydia around 550 BCE. Seeking guidance from the gods whether or not he should fight Cyrus, Croesus sent a messenger to the Oracle at Delphi (DEL-fy), a priestess of Apollo who, it was believed, could tell the future. The problem was that the oracle never gave straightforward answers.

The oracle told Croesus that if he fought Cyrus, "he would destroy a mighty kingdom."[5] Croesus assumed the "mighty kingdom" meant Persia. It was only after Cyrus' army defeated the Lydians and captured Sardis that Croesus realized his mistake: The mighty kingdom was his own.

Croesus worked out an agreement with Cyrus to remain king of Lydia until his death in 546 BCE. After that, Persia took control of Lydia and the rest of its empire. It would remain that way until Alexander the Great destroyed the Persian Empire over two hundred years later. As part of Alexander's empire, the Lydians, along with their customs and language, were slowly assimilated, or absorbed, into the Roman culture.

Theseus, who was born in Troezen, wanted the adventure of traveling overland to meet his father in Athens. He passed through Epidaurus and crossed the Isthmus of Corinth, slaying terrifying monsters on his way. Once he reached Athens, his adventures would take him to Knossos on Crete.

CHAPTER 2
Heir Apparent

Aegeus (EE-jis) was depressed. The king of Athens desperately wanted an heir to take over his throne. He had been married twice but had failed to father a son with either wife. Without an heir, one of his many nephews—whom he considered worthless—would end up ruling Athens. Aegeus and the Athenian people dreaded this possibility.

Aegeus knew all too well that no king was safe from being overthrown, because that's how he came to rule Athens. His father, Pandion II, had been king of Athens until he was exiled from the city after his cousin Metion (MEE-tee-un) seized the throne.

Pandion settled in Megara and married Pylia (PY-lee-uh), the daughter of King Pylas (PY-lus). When Pylas died (or was exiled), Pandion became king of Megara. He and Pylia had four sons: Aegeus, Pallas, Nisus (NIH-suhs) and Lycus (LY-kus). After Pandion died, the brothers returned to Athens and drove out Metion's sons. They reclaimed the city as well as all of Attica, the region of Greece in which Athens and Megara were located.

The brothers divided the control of Attica, but Aegeus, being the eldest, took the most power and became king of Athens. This did not sit well with his brothers or their sons. Athens was considered the most prestigious city in Attica, and Aegeus knew his brothers or nephews would one day try to take it from him, especially if he failed to produce a rightful heir.

Aegeus' first wife was Meta (MEH-tuh). When they were unable to conceive a child, he married Chalciope (kal-SEE-oh-pee). She couldn't get pregnant, either. Fearful of losing his throne and wanting to know

The ancient Greeks believed Delphi was the center of the universe. They marked the spot with a large stone called the omphalos.

if he would ever have a son, he decided to travel to Delphi and consult with the oracle.

The settlement at Delphi was famous for two reasons. First, the Greeks considered it the center of the universe. According to legend, Zeus (ZOOS), the most powerful god, released two eagles from opposite points on earth, and Delphi was where they met. The spot was marked with a large stone called the omphalos (OM-fuh-lus), which means "navel" or "center." Delphi was also home to an oracle, called the Pythia, who foretold the future.

In answer to Aegeus' question about an heir, she responded:

Loose not the wine-skin foot, thou chief of men,
Until to Athens thou art come again.[1]

Aegeus had no idea what she meant. This was not unusual—the Pythia typically spoke in riddles that could be interpreted in a number of different ways. Wanting help to decipher the Pythia's meaning, Aegeus traveled to the city of Troezen (TREH-zen) and visited with his good friend King Pittheus (PIH-thee-us), considered a very wise man.

Pittheus understood that the oracle was warning Aegeus against getting drunk and being with a woman until he was back in Athens. He also figured it meant that Aegeus was going to finally sire a son. Instead of telling Aegeus what he believed the message meant, Pittheus got him drunk, and Aegeus ended up spending the night with Pittheus' daughter Aethra (EE-thruh). In some versions of the story, that same night Aethra went out to the sea, where Poseidon (poh-SY-dun), god of the seas, also made love to her.

Realizing that Aethra might be pregnant from their night together, Aegeus went into the woods and placed a sword and a pair of shoes under a large rock. He told Aethra that if she gave birth to a son, the day he was strong enough to lift the rock and retrieve the sword and shoes was the day she should send the boy to Athens to be with him.

He also cautioned her against telling anybody about their relationship. The historian Plutarch (PLOO-tark) explained the reason: "Aegeus was afraid that [his nephews] might find out about Aethra's child. . . . They were always mutinying against Aegeus' authority and would kill anyone, such as an heir, that might stand between them and supreme power in Athens after Aegeus' death."[2]

As Pittheus had hoped, Aethra did get pregnant—whether the father was Aegeus or Poseidon remained unclear—and gave birth to a healthy boy named Theseus. In many ways, Pittheus was like a father to Theseus, and he made sure the boy was well educated and well cared for. Growing up, Theseus idolized his cousin Heracles (HAYR-uh-kleez) and dreamed of the day he would go on his own adventures. (Hercules [HER-kyoo-leez], the most commonly used variant of the name, was the Roman version of the original Greek name.)

According to tradition, Greek boys let their hair grow long. When they reached puberty, they cut their hair and offered it to the gods. When Theseus was old enough, he went to Delphi, but instead of cutting off all his hair, he cut it short only at the temples and left the rest long. Plutarch explains it was a style worn by the Abantes (ah-BON-teez), a Greek tribe known for its skills.

> The Abantes first used it . . . because they were a warlike people, and used to close fighting, and above all other nations accustomed to engage hand to hand. . . . Therefore that they might not give their enemies a hold by their hair, they cut it in this manner. They write also that this was the reason why

CHAPTER 2

> Alexander gave command to his captains that all the beards of the Macedonians should be shaved, as being the readiest hold for an enemy.[3]

It was clear that Theseus was preparing to be a warrior. Strong and agile, by the time he turned sixteen, Theseus was considered a man. Aethra took her son into the woods and told him where to find the rock. She asked him to lift it and bring her what was underneath. When he came back with the sword and the sandals, she finally told him his father was Aegeus, King of Athens, and that he was heir to the throne.

He was eager to get to Athens but also worried about meeting his powerful father. To impress Aegeus and to prove himself a worthy leader, Theseus decided to walk to Athens rather than sail there on a ship.

Both Aethra and Pittheus were upset about his decision. Travel by road was very dangerous, filled with bandits and killers. But Theseus insisted, inspired by his idol, Heracles, who had rid many areas of criminals in his travels. Theseus felt he needed to be equally tested if he were to earn the respect of his fathers and the people of Athens. As Plutarch relates:

> He thought it therefore a dishonourable thing, and not to be endured, that Heracles should go out everywhere, and purge both land and sea from wicked men, and he himself should fly from the like adventures that actually came in his way.[4]

Theseus said goodbye to his mother and grandfather and left Troezen, ready to follow his destiny.

The Oracle at Delphi

Apollo

The Oracle at Delphi is a religious shrine that dates back to at least 1200 BCE. Located in a cave on Mount Parnassus, it was considered the holiest temple of the ancient Greeks.

The first shrine at Delphi honored Gaia (GY-uh), or Mother Earth. According to Greek myth, that shrine was protected by a giant snake called Python. Apollo, the sun god, killed Python and took over the temple as a shrine for himself. The story symbolizes how Greek civilization evolved from primitive times.

Apollo was also the god of prophecy, or foretelling the future. People would travel to Delphi from all over Greece to find out what the future had in store for them. He spoke through a priestess called the Pythia.

When Apollo's followers arrived at Delphi, they were required to register, then pay money as an offering. After hearing the question, the Pythia would go down into the cave. According to Plutarch, the priestess breathed in fumes rising from the floor of the cave, which put her into a trance. That's when she would communicate with Apollo.[5]

When she relayed what Apollo told her, it was usually very cryptic, like a riddle. If the person was completely confused, the Pythia would offer to provide another prophecy—for an additional fee. Sometimes, the priestess would be overcome by the vapors in the cave and return almost delirious.[6]

For a long time modern historians assumed the fumes were myth. Then scientists discovered there really were gases coming up into the cave from cracks in the stone. Dr. Henry A. Spiller, who helped analyze the gases, explained the effects on the priestesses: "In the first stages, [the gas] produces disembodied euphoria, an altered mental status and a pleasant sensation. . . . The greater the dose, the deeper you go."[7]

Fortunately for the Pythia, once she stopped breathing the gas, the effects quickly disappeared. What Greeks believed was a trance caused by the god Apollo was actually a reaction to poisonous fumes.

The road to Athens was a dangerous place. Theseus believed that in order to be a hero, he had to prove his courage. He successfully defeated giants, robbers, and vicious animals he encountered on his journey, including slaying the Pinebender, Sinis.

CHAPTER 3

The Six Labors

On his way to Athens, Theseus would perform six labors. He had only traveled for a short time when he was faced with his first challenge. Passing through Epidaurus (eh-pih-DAR-us), he ran into a giant named Periphetes (pur-RIH-fuh-teez), whose father was the metalworking god Hephaestus (heh-FES-tus). Like his father, Periphetes also had a lame leg. He used a giant metal club made by Hephaestus as a crutch. He also used it to bash in the heads of people he robbed.

Periphetes approached Theseus, thinking he would be an easy mark because of his slender build. Although Periphetes was much bigger, Theseus was quick and incredibly strong. Managing to grab the club away, he smashed Periphetes in the head with it and killed him. Plutarch describes how Theseus kept the club:

> Being pleased with the club, he took it, and made it his weapon, continuing to use it as Heracles did the lion's skin, on whose shoulders that served to prove how huge a beast he had killed; and to the same end Theseus carried about him this club; overcome indeed by him, but now, in his hands, invincible.[1]

When he was near the Isthmus of Corinth, he encountered another giant, Sinis (SIH-nis), the Bender of Pines. Sinis would kill people by tying their arms and legs to branches of pine trees that had been bent close together and fastened. Once his victim was tied up, he would release the branches, ripping the person apart.

CHAPTER 3

As he had done with Periphetes, Theseus turned the tables on Sinis by tying him to a tree and dismembering him. Theseus was following Heracles' example of eliminating evildoers by making them suffer the same way their victims did. Legend has it that, years later, Theseus commemorated his victory over Sinis by instituting an athletic festival called the Isthmian Games.

Before continuing his journey, Theseus tracked down Sinis' beautiful daughter Perigune (puh-RIH-guh-nee), who had run away after her father was killed. He promised not to kill her but forced her to spend the night with him. She later gave birth to Theseus' first son, Melanippus (meh-luh-NIH-pus).

Even though Theseus was pleased to have defeated two criminals who happened to cross his path, he didn't think it was enough to merely defend himself against attack. To be a hero like Heracles, he also needed to test himself against worthy animal adversaries. He took a detour to look for Phaea (FAY-uh), a vicious wild sow that was terrifying the town of Crommyon. (In other versions of the story, Phaea was the name of a woman robber who was referred to as a sow because of her wicked lifestyle and manners.)

After killing the beast, Theseus continued on his way to Athens. When he passed through Megara, Aegeus' hometown, he learned it was the home of Sciron (SKY-ron). An elderly robber, Sciron made people wash his feet, then he would kick them over a cliff into the ocean, where they would be eaten by a huge turtle. When the old man tried to get Theseus to wash his feet, the hero picked him up and tossed him over the precipice.

Not too far outside of Athens was Eleusis (eh-LYOO-sis), the site of a famous religious festival that honored the goddess Demeter (DIH-mih-ter), who had taught the Greeks how to grow corn. King Cercyon (SUR-see-on), a cruel man, was feared by all his subjects. He had his daughter Alope (AL-oh-pee) buried alive for having a child, Hippothoon (hih-PAH-thoo-on), with Poseidon. The god honored Alope by turning her into a spring, or natural fountain.

Cercyon was also a man of great strength. He would challenge passers-by to a wrestling match. If they beat him, they would inherit Eleusis and get to be king. If they lost, he killed them as a sacrifice to the gods. When Theseus came into Eleusis, the citizens begged him not to wrestle Cercyon, convinced he would die like all the others. Theseus confronted the king anyway. Author Charles Kingsley described how the match would have gone:

> So they tossed off all their garments, and went forth in the palace-yard . . . and there stood face to face, while their eyes glared like wild bulls' and all the people crowded at the gates to see what would befall.
>
> And there they stood and wrestled, till the stars shone out above their heads; up and down and round, till the sand was stamped hard beneath their feet. And their eyes flashed like stars in the darkness, and their breath went up like smoke in the night air; but neither took nor gave a footstep, and the people watched silent at the gates.[2]

The longer Theseus prolonged the match, the angrier it made Cercyon. He throttled Theseus by the neck but could not knock him down. Theseus grabbed Cercyon by his waist and slammed him to the ground with such force that his heard burst, killing him. Eleusis now belonged to Theseus, and he appointed Hippothoon to serve as king.

One of the more gruesome encounters Theseus experienced on his way to Athens was with the giant Procrustes (proh-KRUS-teez), also known as Damastes. This robber had a house close to the road. When he saw travelers passing by, he would invite them to come in for dinner and to rest. Those who accepted were offered his special bed, which he claimed was always the perfect length for whoever was lying on it. Anyone unfortunate enough to get into the bed soon discovered what exactly was so special about it—Procrustes could

Theseus stands before King Aegeus and Queen Medea. When Theseus arrived in Athens, he kept his identity a secret at first. Later, when Aegeus saw Theseus' sword—a sword Aegeus had left with Aethra—he knew Theseus was his son.

personally adjust it. Whenever he saw a potential victim approaching, he would change the length to make sure it wouldn't fit. If someone was too short, Procrustes put him on a rack to stretch him out until he fit. If he was too long for the bed, the giant cut off his victim's legs.

Once again, Theseus meted out his preferred justice by putting Procrustes on the bed. He made the monster fit by cutting off his legs—and his head. The people living nearby thanked Theseus for ridding their area from such a terrible robber.

Outside of Athens was the Cephisus (seh-FY-sus) River, the longest in Attica, where the Phytalidae (fy-TAH-lih-dy) lived. They were descendants of the hero King Phytalus (FY-tuh-lus) of Eleusis, who once helped Demeter. In return, she gave Phytalus the fig tree. Theseus asked the Phytalidae to purify him from all the blood he had shed on his journey. They were happy to honor Theseus and performed a ritual that included offerings to Zeus. Spiritually cleansed, Theseus was ready to face his father in Athens.

By this time Aegeus, now an old man, was married yet again. His new wife was the powerful sorceress, or witch, Medea (mee-DEE-uh). She was not a woman to mess with. Her father Aeëtes (ee-EE-teez), the king of Colchis (KOHL-kis), had owned the golden fleece. When Jason came to steal the fleece, Medea fell in love with him and helped him against her father.

She and Jason married and had two children. Years later, Jason left Medea to marry another woman, and Medea plotted a horrible revenge. First she murdered his new wife. To make him suffer even more, she killed her own two children and fled to Athens, where Aegeus offered her refuge. In return, she promised to use her magic to bear him a son. Aegeus agreed and they were married. As Roman poet Ovid would later observe:

> Here Aegeus so engaging she addrest,
> That first he treats her like a royal guest;
> Then takes the sorc'ress for his wedded wife;
> The only blemish of his prudent life.[3]

Although some suspected the natural father was not Aegeus, Medea gave birth to a son, Medus (MEE-dus). She plotted for him be the next king of Athens.

When Theseus arrived in Athens, he was shocked to find the city in turmoil. Different factions, or groups, were jostling for power rather than working together to make Athens a better place to live. However, everyone greeted Theseus warmly. News of his deeds had already reached the city, so he was hailed as a hero for making the road to Athens safe again from killers and robbers.

CHAPTER 3

Medea immediately sensed Theseus was a threat to her son's claim on the throne. Knowing that Aegeus worried constantly about being overthrown by one of his nephews, she played on the king's fears. Medea convinced Aegeus that Theseus was in Athens to take the throne away from him. The only way to stay in power was to kill Theseus. Aegeus fell for the lie.

Theseus was invited to a banquet at Aegeus' home. When he got there, he decided to keep his identity a secret a while longer. He hoped his father would eventually recognize who he was. When everyone sat down to eat, Theseus was given some wine to drink. It was laced with poison. As he put his sword on the table, Aegeus realized Theseus was his son. He immediately knocked the cup away and embraced him. Furious at Medea, Aegeus went to kill her, but she used her magic to get away, fleeing with Medus back to Colchis.

When Aegeus revealed Theseus' identity and announced he was the rightful heir to the throne, the citizens of Athens cheered. The only people not happy were Aegeus' brother Pallas and his sons. Determined to gain control of the throne, they broke up into two groups. The first, led by Pallas, marched on Athens. The second group planned to ambush Theseus. Theseus was tipped off and killed his attackers. When Pallas and the rest of his sons heard, they abandoned their attack and ran away.

Theseus had saved his father and proved himself a worthy leader. And his adventures were just beginning.

The Panhellenic Games

Chariot racing

The Isthmian Games were one of four athletic festivals that together were known as the Panhellenic Games. The other competitions were the Nemean (nuh-MAY-un) Games, The Pythian Games, and the Olympic Games. Held near Corinth, these games honored Poseidon.

The contests rotated on a four-year cycle called the Olympiad. The Olympics took place in Year 1; the Nemean and Isthmian Games in Year 2; the Pythian Games in Year 3; and the Nemean and Isthmian Games again in Year 4. Then the Olympiad started over again with the Olympics.

One reason for staggering the festivals was so that athletes could compete in all the different games. The Isthmian Games attracted participants from all over Greece and its colonies, which spanned from the Middle East to Spain. Most of the athletes came from noble or wealthy families. A peasant would not be able to afford the cost of transportation, housing, food, and other expenses. Only Greek men were allowed to participate.

Among the competitions were boxing, chariot racing, wrestling, running races, and the pentathlon, a combined event that included wrestling, javelin, discus, long jump, and stadion, a footrace covering about 200 yards. There were also nonathletic competitions in the arts such as music and drama.

One of the most popular sports was pankration (pan-KRAY-shun). Similar to modern-day ultimate fighting, it was believed to have been cofounded by Heracles and Theseus. Introduced in 648 BCE, it was a mixture of boxing, kicking, and wrestling that was brutal and occasionally fatal. There were no weight or size classifications, no time limits, and only two rules: no biting and no gouging with fingernails. At local competitions, the rugged Spartans didn't even bother with those rules. Not surprisingly, injuries such as broken limbs were common. A match was over when one of the contestants quit, got knocked out, or died. Because quitting was rare, the match often ended with one of the participants unconscious or hurt too badly to continue. The winner would be awarded a crown of celery.

The Minotaur was a terrifying half-man, half-bull monster that lived on the island of Crete. Every nine years Athens was forced to send fourteen young people to Crete to be sacrificed to the Minotaur. Theseus volunteered to go. Once there, he killed the monster.

THESEUS

CHAPTER 4
The Minotaur

Even though Theseus had earned the respect of the Athenian citizens, he was eager to seek out more adventures. His next mission was to fight the bull of Marathon, which was terrorizing a coastal area known as Ionia (eye-OH-nee-uh). But this was no ordinary bull. When Minos (MY-nohs) wanted to be king of Crete, the people demanded a sign from the gods to prove him worthy. He asked Poseidon to send a bull that would appear from the waves, and in return he would sacrifice the bull to honor the god. Poseidon agreed to the deal, but Minos kept the bull and sacrificed a different one. In some versions, it was Minos' wife, Pasiphae (pah-SIH-fuh-ee), who talked her husband out of sacrificing the proper bull.

Angry, Poseidon punished Minos. First he made the bull vicious. Then he made Pasiphae fall in love with the bull. She got pregnant by the bull and gave birth to the Minotaur (MIH-nuh-tar), a beast that was half man, half bull. Minos hired a famous architect named Daedalus (DAY-duh-lus) to build a labyrinth under the palace. The labyrinth would house the Minotaur—and according to some stories, Pasiphae lived there as well.

Ironically, it was Heracles—Theseus' personal hero—who captured the bull when it was rampaging through Crete. He took it to Greece and set it free, where it roamed until settling in Marathon. Theseus again wanted to follow in his cousin's footsteps and conquer the beast. Instead of killing the bull, Theseus captured it alive and brought it back to Athens for the people to see. Then he sacrificed it to Apollo. (Some sources tell the story of Theseus and the bull as occurring earlier, as a trick of Medea before she poisoned his wine.) Soon, Athenians were filled with dread because the time had come

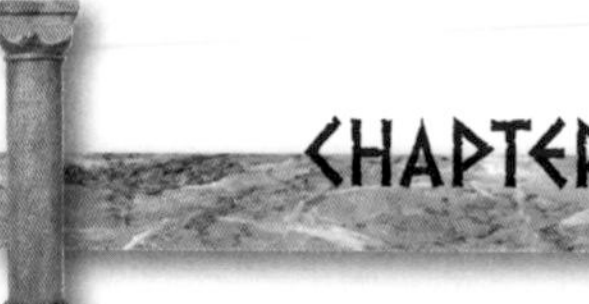

CHAPTER 4

Mestrius Plutarchus, better known today as Plutarch, was a Greek historian and biographer. Born in 46 CE into a wealthy family, Plutarch is best known for his book *Parallel Lives*, which tells the biographies, both real and legendary, of famous Greeks and Romans.

for Aegeus to send a number of young people to Crete to be sacrificed to the Minotaur. The gruesome practice was a debt Aegeus owed Minos over the death of his son, Androgeos (an-DROH-jee-us).

Years earlier, Androgeos traveled to Athens to participate in some athletic contests. A gifted athlete, he won all his competitions. Some stories claim Aegeus was upset that Androgeos had made the Athenian athletes look bad. Others suggest he was worried Androgeos

would join forces with Aegeus' nephews and overthrow him. Whatever his reasons, Aegeus saw to it that the young man was killed. King Minos was beside himself with grief and vowed revenge. Plutarch recounts that the gods were not happy with Aegeus, either:

> Androgeos having been treacherously murdered in the confines of Attica, not only Minos, his father, put the Athenians to extreme distress by a perpetual war, but the gods also laid waste their country; both famine and pestilence lay heavy upon them, and even their rivers were dried up. Being told by the oracle that, if they appeased and reconciled Minos, the anger of the gods would cease and they should enjoy rest from the miseries they labored under.[1]

So it was agreed that every nine years, Aegeus would send seven young men and seven virgin girls to Crete. What happened to these youths differs according to the stories. Some thought they were sacrificed by being put in the labyrinth with the Minotaur, who would eat them. Others suggested that they were let loose in the labyrinth and, unable to get out, died of starvation and lack of water. In Minoan lore, they ended up slaves, given to the winners of games put on by King Minos.

Regardless of whether they were eaten, left to die, or enslaved, Theseus was determined to put an end to the practice. If the Minotaur could be destroyed, the debt would end. So when it came time for the third group of Athenians to be sent to Crete, Theseus volunteered to be included. Not only was it the kind of adventure he sought out—the chance to confront and kill the Minotaur—he was also doing it out of duty. Who went to Crete was determined by a lottery, and parents would wail with grief if their child was unfortunate enough to be among those chosen. As the son of Aegeus, Theseus had to go. Plutarch describes his choice:

> The Athenians grumbled that Aegeus, who was the cause of their trouble, would not participate in the lottery, and that true Athenians sacrificed their children so a foreign bastard might inherit the kingdom.
>
> Theseus was aware of this discontent, so he offered himself as one of the victims, not just as a participant in the lottery. Everyone admired the nobility and loved the goodness of this act, and all of Aegeus' tears could not turn Theseus away from his noble resolution.[2]

Once the other youths were picked, the Athenians would set sail for Crete. As was done the previous two times, the ship was fitted with a black sail, symbolic of both the grief of the families and the hopelessness of those being sacrificed. But Theseus, showing confidence and maybe a little cockiness, promised to put a white sail on the ship when it returned—as a signal to Aegeus that he was alive and had successfully killed the Minotaur.

After making an offering to Apollo of an olive branch wrapped in wool, Theseus was ready to leave. When the Athenians arrived in Crete, they were brought before King Minos. With him was his daughter Ariadne (ayr-ee-AD-nee), who fell in love with Theseus at first sight. To make sure her new love wasn't killed by the Minotaur, Ariadne secretly helped him. She gave him a sword and a length of thread, which he could use to find his way back out of the labyrinth.[3]

There has been debate over whether the structure Daedalus built was a true labyrinth, which normally has one path leading to the center, or a maze, which is filled with dead ends and has an entrance and an exit. The details notwithstanding, Theseus found his way. Symbolically, the labyrinth represents the journey Theseus took to free the Athenians from being under the thumb of Crete.

Plutarch also recounts Philochorus (fih-LAH-kuh-rus), a Greek historian who tells a much less fanciful sequence of events. According

to Philochorus, Minos held games that were always won by Taurus, one of the king's powerful captains. Instead of being a national hero, the people of Crete hated Taurus because he was cruel and crude. Minos wasn't overly fond of him either, because he was worried Taurus wanted to steal away Pasiphae. When the Athenians arrived, Theseus stepped forward and requested to compete with Taurus. Minos agreed.

Theseus beat Taurus in athletic combat, humiliating him. Minos was so pleased and impressed, he waived the debt and allowed the Athenians to go home instead of staying in Crete as slaves. Ariadne was so swept away by Theseus that she left with him to go back to Athens. Some say he promised to marry her.

Both versions of the story emphasize Athens' ability to overcome challenges posed by Crete, which for many years was the most advanced culture in the region. It signified Athens' growing importance, which set the stage for the city's rise as a Greek power.

Theseus' triumph came at a great cost for the two people who loved him most. On his way back to Athens, Theseus stopped off at the island of Naxos for supplies and to let the ship's crew and passengers rest. When he set sail again for Athens, he left Ariadne behind. Nobody knew why. Some traditions hold that while on the island, Theseus had a dream in which he was told that the god Dionysus (dy-uh-NY-sus) had fallen in love with Ariadne; he left her so that she could live out her life as the god's wife on Mount Olympus. Other stories have a much less happy ending. They say she hanged herself after being abandoned by the man for whom she had betrayed her father and country.

As they neared Athens, Theseus was so excited to return home that he forgot to have the sail changed from black to white. When the ship came into view from the shore and Aegeus saw the black sail, he thought his son was dead. In despair, he killed himself by jumping off a cliff into the water. In honor of him, the sea became known as the Aegean.

Theseus arrived in Athens to find the citizens grieving. He was heartbroken to realize his forgetfulness had resulted in his father's death. When his brother Pallas heard about Aegeus' death, he tried to organize an uprising to take the throne. But Theseus killed Pallas and was crowned king of Athens.

Plutarch reported that the ship used to carry Theseus to and from Crete was preserved as a historical monument for 900 years, into the third century BCE:

> The ship wherein Theseus and the youth of Athens returned had thirty oars, and was preserved by the Athenians . . . for they took away the old planks as they decayed, putting in new and stronger timber in their place.[4]

After a while, every plank of wood in the ship had been replaced, prompting philosophers to argue whether or not the ship could really be called Theseus' anymore, since none of the original wood remained. The question is still considered a philosophical conundrum, known as the Ship of Theseus, about how much an object can change before it is no longer what it once was.

One thing nobody would argue is that once he became king, Theseus changed the course of Greek history.

Minoan Civilization

The Minoan Palace of Knossos

The Minoan civilization evolved on the island of Crete around 3000 BCE, and the Minoans were the dominant culture in the Aegean region for many centuries. A peaceful people, they were skilled sailors and successful merchants. By comparison, Mycenaean cities like Athens were very weak economically.

Being an island culture, the Minoans particularly worshiped the sea god Poseidon. They also revered the bull, a symbol of strength. One of their favorite sports was bull leaping: Young athletes would grab a bull's horns and flip themselves over the animal.

In 1700 BCE, a powerful earthquake struck Crete, destroying all the royal palaces. They were quickly rebuilt bigger and better than before. The largest and most famous palace was located in Knossos (kuh-NOH-sus), the Minoans' greatest city. The building was extremely advanced for its time. The king and queen enjoyed bathtubs, toilets, and running water.

It was also huge, with hundreds of rooms within its four levels, which surrounded a central courtyard. The palace at Knossos has been described as being like a labyrinth because there were many hallways that led to the same place. Some historians believe that the design of the palace might have been the inspiration for the story of the labyrinth, or that the labyrinth symbolized the palace itself.

The most famous ruler of Crete was King Minos, but many historians believe that the word *minos* was just another term for king. There could have been many Minoses, just as there were many pharaohs who ruled Egypt.

The Minoan civilization thrived until around 1450 BCE. Eventually, all the palaces were destroyed by fire except for the great palace of Knossos. Although archaeologists are unsure what caused the fires, it is suspected that the Greeks burned the island when they conquered the Minoans sometime during in the fifteenth century BCE. The story of Theseus, then, directly represents the shift in power from the Minoans to the Mycenaeans, when the Greek city-states began to emerge as the new powers of the Aegean region.

Hippolytus, who favors Artemis, virgin goddess of the hunt, stands before Theseus and Phaedra. He is the son of Theseus and his first wife, Hippolyte, Queen of the Amazons. After Hippolytus was born, Theseus married Phaedre, whose father was Crete's King Minos. According to legend, Aphrodite put a spell on Phaedre to make her fall in love with her stepson, but Hippolytus refused her romantic advances.

CHAPTER 5

Theseus' Legacy

As king, Theseus set in motion an ambitious plan to make Athens more powerful. First, he persuaded the inhabitants of Attica to become part of the Athens city-state—in essence making them all Athenians. He promised local leaders that he would give up the monarchy in favor of a people-run government. In other words, Theseus instituted a democracy, and his job in the new system would be to command the army and to make sure laws were followed. As Plutarch tells us:

> He then dissolved all the distinct statehouses, council halls, and magistracies, and built one common state-house and council hall on the site of the present upper town, and gave the name of Athens to the whole state. . . . Then, as he had promised, he laid down his regal power and proceeded to order a commonwealth.[1]

Once his reforms were in place, Theseus left Athens and traveled to the land of the Amazons, a race of female warriors descended from Ares, the god of war. There is a lot of disagreement over this story. Some stories claim that Theseus accompanied Heracles on his ninth labor to retrieve the belt of the Amazon queen. (Heracles was given twelve labors, or tasks, to atone for killing his wife and children. If he succeeded, he was promised immortality by the gods.) However, most of the stories say that Theseus traveled to the land of the Amazons simply seeking adventure.

When he arrived, the queen of the Amazons, Hippolyte (hih-PAH-luh-tee), greeted Theseus warmly. In return, he kidnapped her and set sail for Athens, claiming her as his bride. In other stories, when

Theseus is accompanying Heracles, the queen is identified an Antiope (an-TEE-oh-pee). To confuse matters more, other stories identify Antiope as Hippolyte's sister.

What is agreed is that when their queen was kidnapped, the Amazons waged war on Athens. When neither side could defeat the other, they declared a truce, and the Amazons left. Theseus married Hippolyte, and they had a son named Hippolytus (hih-PAH-lih-tus).

Eventually, Theseus married Phaedra (FAY-druh), who happened to be King Minos' daughter and the sister of Ariadne. Some stories say that Theseus dumped Hippolyte; others that she had died, possibly in childbirth, before he took Phaedra as his wife.

In Euripides' play *Hippolytus*, Aphrodite, the goddess of love, becomes angry after Hippolytus spurns her "spell and seeks no woman's kiss."[2] Like his Amazon mother, he has absolutely no interest in the opposite sex and is happiest while he's hunting. Aphrodite gets her revenge by having his stepmother, Phaedra, fall in love with him. When Hippolytus refuses her advances, Phaedra kills herself. Unaware of Aphrodite's part, in her suicide note she blames Hippolytus for making her fall in love. Outraged, Theseus makes a plea to Poseidon:

> Poseidon! Thou didst grant me for mine own
> Three prayers; for one of these, slay now my son,
> Hippolytus; let him not outlive this day . . .[3]

Artemis (AR-tuh-mis), the goddess of the hunt, tells Theseus the truth, but it's too late. Poseidon has sent a monster to scare Hippolytus' horses. They run him over, and he is dying. He forgives his father with his dying words, but Theseus is consumed by grief that he has caused his son's death. As a crowd carries the body of Hippolytus into the palace, the people say:

A grief hath fallen beyond men's fears.
There cometh a throbbing of many tears,
A sound as of waters falling.
For when great men die,
A mighty name and a bitter cry
Rise up from a nation calling.[4]

The moral of Euripides' play is that tragedy is sure to befall anyone who lacks balance in his or her life. Human affection and ambition need to coexist for a truly successful existence. And it would be Theseus' self-indulgent ambition that would prove his downfall.

Many years before Phaedra's death, Theseus met Peirithous (py-RIH-thoh-us), the king of the Lapiths—a tribe that lived in Thessaly, a region in central Greece. Peirithous wanted to test the stories about the courage and strength of Theseus, so he decided to try to steal some of Theseus' cattle. Theseus caught him but, Plutarch says, didn't punish him.

> When these two warriors faced each other, each of them admired the strength and courage of the other, and lost all desire to fight. . . . Theseus not only pardoned Perithous but also proposed that they become brothers-in-arms. Then and there, they took the oath.[5]

Peirithous and Theseus became best friends, but they were not good influences on each other. Soon after Theseus became a widower, Peirithous' wife also died. The two kings decided that they should each marry a daughter of Zeus and worked together to fulfill that goal. Peirithous helped Theseus kidnap Helen of Sparta—the same Helen who would later set off the Trojan War—when she was only twelve. Theseus, by then fifty years old, gave the girl to his mother, Aethra, for safekeeping. The men then went to kidnap Persephone (per-SEH-fuh-nee), the wife of Hades (HAY-deez), god of the

Underworld. Hades learned of the plan and imprisoned them in Tartarus (TAR-tuh-rus)—a place in the Underworld reserved for particularly harsh punishment. He bound them to a chair for eternity. Heracles was able to rescue Theseus after asking Hades to spare his cousin. But Peirithous remained in Tartarus.

In the meantime, Helen's twin brothers, Castor and Polydeuces (pah-lih-DOO-seez), who were also called the Dioscuri (dy-uh-SKYOO-ree), traveled to Athens and threatened to attack the city if their sister wasn't returned. The Athenians had no idea what Theseus had done, but war was averted when they figured out where Helen was being kept.

The people of Athens were upset with Theseus. In his absence, a nobleman named Menestheus (meh-NES-thee-us) emerged as a leader, gaining support by turning people against Theseus. By the time Theseus returned, he was no longer considered a hero. Rather than try to take back his leadership of Athens through war, he left and sailed to the island Scyros (SKEE-ros), where he was welcomed by King Lycomedes (ly-KOH-muh-deez), an old friend of Aegeus.

The former hero had fallen so out of favor that few people cared when news of his death spread. Some stories claim he slipped and fell when walking near a cliff. Other says that in order to gain favor with Menestheus, Lycomedes pushed him over it. Menestheus became king and Theseus was forgotten for half a millennium—until the Battle of Marathon.

When reports of Theseus' ghost leading the soldiers into battle reached Athens, the Oracle at Delphi was consulted. It instructed that Theseus' bones be brought back to Athens. In 475 BCE, an Athenian general named Cimon (SIH-mon), Miltiades' son, found some human remains that he believed were those of Theseus. He brought the relics back to Athens to be buried in the center of the city.

His tomb is a sanctuary and refuge for slaves and all those of mean condition who fly from the persecution of men in power.

Cimon was an Athenian politician and general. His father was Miltiades, who led the Greek army against the Persians in the Battle of Marathon. Cimon brought Theseus' remains back to Athens for burial.

It reminds them that Theseus, while he lived, was an assister and protector of the distressed, and never refused the petitions of the afflicted that fled to him.[6]

The story of Theseus embodies both the most noble achievements of man—protecting others and devoting oneself to public service—and the disastrous consequences of pride and indulgence. It is one thing to achieve power and greatness, quite another to maintain it. As Athens evolved from a second-class city into one of the most influential cultures the world has ever known, figures such as Theseus were forgotten as remnants of the past. It was only later that the people of Athens began to better appreciate their beginning history and the oral traditions passed down over the centuries of the heroes who helped create that history.

Whether or not there was really a historical king named Theseus isn't as important as what his story represents: the transition of Athens into an advanced civilization that embraced the importance of the individual citizen. Through that democratic ideal, ancient Athens—and its heroes—remain immortal like the gods, living on through its legacy of political, scientific, and literary accomplishments.

The Amazons

Amazon warrior vase

The Amazons were a tribe of warrior women. Their only contact with men was to mate with them. They would kill any boys born but would raise daughters to be warriors.

Like a lot of stories that were long considered completely fictional, historians now believe that the many tales in Greek mythology about the Amazons may have a strong basis in fact. The question of just who these warrior women were and where they came from has been argued for literally thousands of years. Plutarch believed that the Amazons weren't a separate race but were merely fictionalized accounts of women soldiers fighting alongside men. For example, in his time it was known that in some Germanic tribes, women accompanied men into battle. And fourth century BCE burial sites have been excavated that contain women buried with armor and weapons, indicating they died in battle.

In the late 1990s, archaeologists working near Pokrovka, Russia, unearthed over 150 burial mounds from the fifth century BCE. Many contained women buried with armor and weapons. Jeannine Davis-Kimball, Director of the Center for the Study of Eurasian Nomads in Berkeley, California, told *The Washington Post* an arrowhead was found in the body of one woman, "suggesting that she had been killed in battle. . . . These finds suggest that Greek tales of Amazon warriors may have had some basis in fact,"[7] and may have been the inspiration for the many legends.

According to Herodotus,[8] after the Greeks beat the Amazons at Thermodon (THER-muh-don), they sailed back to Greece with three ships of Amazon prisoners. The Amazons revolted and killed their guards. Not knowing how to sail, they drifted until they came ashore and encountered the Scyths, a Eurasian tribe. The Scyths were so impressed with the Amazons, they wanted to marry them to produce children with superior fighting skills. The resulting race of nomadic people were the Sarmatians (sar-MAY-shuns). Their society was matriarchal, or run by women, and there is archaeological evidence they emerged around 600 BCE—from the same time period as the Pokrovka burial grounds.

As with many stories in Greek history, myth and fact are often impossible to separate.

CHRONOLOGY

Dates before 776 BCE are approximate and by tradition

BCE

3000 Minoan civilization emerges in Crete.

1309 Pandion becomes King of Athens.

1282 Pandion dies.

1286 Heracles is born.

1284 In Athens, Aegeus wins power back from Metions' sons.

1271 Theseus is born.

1270 Androgeos is killed.

1256 Theseus leaves for Athens and performs six labors.

1252 Theseus kills the Minotaur.

1235 Towns of Attica join to form Athens city-state.

1221 Theseus abducts Helen; he is imprisoned in Tartarus by Hades.

1207 Theseus is freed from the Underworld by Heracles.

1206 Theseus dies.

1203 Helen is abducted by Paris, setting off the Trojan War.

1183 Troy falls.

776 First Olympiad takes place.

640 First coins are produced in Lydia.

581 Isthmian Games are established.

490 Battle of Marathon is fought.

484 Herodotus is born.

428 Euripides writes Hippolytus.

TIMELINE

Dates are approximate.

BCE

2550 Cheops begins building the Great Pyramid in Egypt.

2500 *The Epic of Gilgamesh*, the oldest known book, is written in Sumeria.

2000 Phoenicians develop the alphabet.

1780 Code of Hammurabi is established.

1600 Shang Dynasty starts in China.

1645 One of the most powerful volcanic eruptions ever occurs on Thera in the Aegean Sea.

1325 King Tut dies.

1200 Corn is introduced from Mexico into what is now the southwestern United States.

1292 Ramses II becomes Pharaoh.

1010 David becomes King of Israel

1000 The kite is invented in China.

800 Indian mathematician Baudhayana develops theorem of what is now known as Pythagorean equation: $a^2 + b^2 = c^2$

753 Rome is founded.

750 The *Iliad* is put in writing.

563 Siddhartha Gautama, also known as Buddha, is born.

551 Confucius is born.

429 Outbreak of the plague kills one-third of Athens' population.

356 Alexander the Great is born.

CHAPTER NOTES

Chapter 1. Battle of Marathon

1. George Grote, *A History of Greece: From the Time of Solon to 403 BCE*, M.O.B. Caspari and J. M. Mitchell, eds. (London: Routledge, 2001), p. 185.

2. Herodotus Texts, *The History of Herodotus*, translated by G. C. Macaulay, M.A., Book 6, 105, http://ancienthistory.about.com/library/bl/bl_text_herodotus_6.htm

3. Herotodus, *The History of Herodotus*, translated by David Grene (Chicago: University of Chicago Press, 1987), p. 454.

4. Ibid. pp. 455–456.

5. Herodotus, *The History of Herodotus*, translated by George Rawlinson, Book I, line 91. http://classics.mit.edu/Herodotus/history.1.i.html

Chapter 2. Heir Apparent

1. Plutarch, *Theseus*, translated by John Dryden (New York: Biblo and Tannen, 1966), http://classics.mit.edu/Plutarch/theseus.html

2. Ibid.

3. Plutarch, *Plutarch's Lives*, edited by John S. White (New York: Biblo and Tannen, 1966), p. 8.

4. Plutarch, *Theseus*.

5. Plutarch, "On the Cessation of Oracles," http://thriceholy.net/Texts/Oracles.html

6. Ibid.

7. William Broad, "For Delphic Oracle, Fumes and Visions," *New York Times*, *Science Times*, Tuesday, March 19, 2002, pp. D1, D4.

Chapter 3. The Six Labors

1. Plutarch, *Plutarch's Lives*, edited by John S. White (New York: Biblo and Tannen, 1966), p. 8.

2. Charles Kingley, *The Heroes* (London: J.M. Dent & Company, 1899), p. 151.

3. Ovid, *Metamorphoses*, Book VII, The Internet Classics Archive, http://classics.mit.edu/Ovid/metam.7.seventh.html

Chapter 4. The Minotaur

1. Plutarch, *Theseus*, translated by John Dryden (New York: Biblo and Tannen, 1966), http://classics.mit.edu/Plutarch/theseus.html

2. Plutarch, *Theseus*, The Athenian Adventurer, http://www.e-classics.com/theseus.htm

3. Thomas Bulfinch, *The Age of Fable* (New York: Review of Reviews, 1913; Bartleby.com, 2000), http://www.bartleby.com/bulfinch

4. Plutarch, *Plutarch's Lives*, edited by John S. White (New York: Biblo and Tannen, 1966), p. 17.

Chapter 5. Theseus' Legacy

1. Plutarch, *Theseus*, translated by John Dryden (New York: Biblo and Tannen, 1966), http://classics.mit.edu/Plutarch/theseus.html

2. Euripides, *Hippolytus*, translated by Gilbert Murray, Vol. VIII, Part 7 (The Harvard Classics, New York: P.F. Collier & Son, 1909–14; Bartleby.com, 2001), http://www.bartleby.com/8/7/, line 15.

3. Ibid., lines 947–949.

4. Ibid., lines 1595–1601.

5. Plutarch, *Theseus*, The Athenian Adventurer, http://www.e-classics.com/theseus.htm

6. Plutarch, *Plutarch's Lives*, edited by John S. White (New York: Biblo and Tannen, 1966), pp. 26–27.

7. Kathy Sawyer, "Were Amazons More than Myths?" *The Washington Post*, May 19, 1997.

8. Herodotus, *The History of Herodotus*, translated by George Rawlinson, http://www.fordham.edu/halsall/ancient/herodotus-history.txt

FURTHER READING

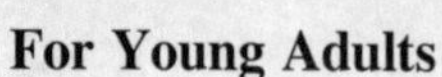

For Young Adults

Fisher, Leonard Everett. *Theseus and the Minotaur*. New York: Holiday House, 1992.

McCaughrean, Geraldine. *Theseus (Heroes)*. Chicago: Cricket Books; 2005.

McMullan, Kate. *Myth-O-Mania: Stop That Bull, Theseus!* New York: Volo, 2003.

Works Consulted

Bernard, Suzanne. *Plato & His Dialogues: Theseus, Legendary King of Athens* http://plato-dialogues.org/tools/char/theseus.htm

Broad, William. "For Delphic Oracle, Fumes and Visions." *New York Times*, Science Times, Tuesday, March 19, 2002. pp. D1, D4.

Bulfinch, Thomas. *The Age of Fable*. New York: Review of Reviews, 1913; Bartleby.com, 2000. http://www.bartleby.com/bulfinch

Euripides. *Hippolytus,* translated by Gilbert Murray. Vol. VIII, Part 7. The Harvard Classics. New York: P.F. Collier & Son, 1909–14; Bartleby.com, 2001. http://www.bartleby.com/8/7/

Grote, George. *A History of Greece: From the Time of Solon to 403 BCE*. M.O.B. Caspari and J. M. Mitchell, eds. London: Routledge, 2001.

Herodotus. *The History of Herodotus*. Translated by G. C. Macaulay, M.A. http://ancienthistory.about.com/library/bl/bl_text_herodotus_6.htm

Herotodus. *The History of Herodotus*. Translated by David Grene. Chicago: University of Chicago Press, 1987.

Herodotus. *The History of Herodotus*. Translated by George Rawlinson. http://www.fordham.edu/halsall/ancient/herodotus-history.txt

Kingsley, Charles. *The Heroes*. London: J.M. Dent & Company, 1899.

Plutarch. "On the Cessation of Oracles." http://thriceholy.net/Texts/Oracles.html

Plutarch. *Plutarch's Lives*. John S. White, ed. New York: Biblo and Tannen, 1966.

Price, Simon. "Delphi and Divination." *Greek Religion & Society*. Cambridge: Easterling & Muir, 1985.

Sawyer, Kathy. "Were Amazons More than Myths?" *The Washington Post,* May 19, 1997.

Walker, Henry J. *Theseus and Athens*. New York: Oxford University Press, 1995.

On the Internet

Greek History for Kids, Ancient Greeks http://www.historyforkids.org/learn/greeks/index.htm

History for Kids, *The Lydians*, http://www.historyforkids.org/learn/westasia/history/lydians.htm

The Internet Classics Archives, *Theseus by Plutarch*, translated by John Dryden, http://classics.mit.edu/Plutarch/theseus.html

conundrum (kuh-NUN-drum)—A riddle or difficult problem.

electrum (ee-LEK-trum)—A naturally occurring mixture, or alloy, of gold and silver.

exile (EK-syl)—To banish someone from his or her country.

faction (FAK-shun)—A group that splits off from a main group.

isthmus (ISS-mus)—A narrow strip of land, with water on both sides, that connects two larger landmasses.

labyrinth (LAH-brinth)—A complex passageway whose exit can be difficult to find. It is different from a maze because mazes are filled with many paths that dead-end, while labyrinths usually have a single path.

mercenary (MUR-seh-nay-ree)—A person who fights with a foreign army for money.

precipice (PREH-suh-pis)—A very steep cliff.

Pythia (PIH-thee-uh)—The priestess who served as the oracle at Delphi.

tyrant (TY-runt)—To the Greeks, a leader who had no real legal right to rule but whose authority was forced upon them. The term did not necessarily mean that the ruler was unjust or brutal.

widower (WIH-doh-er)—A man whose wife has died.

INDEX